Sufi Poetry

Sufi Poetry

Prophecy and Persian Sufi Poetry

Gender Inclusive Edition
Adapted into Modern English

Hazrat
Pir-o-Murshid
Inayat Khan

Edited and Annotated by
Pir Netanel Miles-Yépez

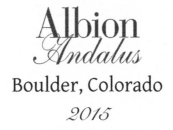

Boulder, Colorado
2015

"The old shall be renewed,
and the new shall be made holy."
— Rabbi Avraham Yitzhak Kook

Albion-Andalus, Inc.
P. O. Box 19852
Boulder, CO 80308
www.albionandalus.com

Cover design by Daryl McCool
Design and layout by Albion-Andalus Books
"Rose-Heart and Wings" illustration
© 2008 Netanel Miles-Yépez

Manufactured in the United States of America

ISBN-13: 978-0692428528 (Albion-Andalus Books)
ISBN-10: 0692428526

CONTENTS

EDITOR'S PREFACE

HAZRAT INAYAT KHAN was himself a poet and musician, uniquely qualified to talk about Sufi poetry from both an artistic and spiritual perspective. This slim book, simply entitled, *Sufi Poetry,* is a collection of talks by the master on the Persian Sufi poets and the mystical connection between poetry and prophecy. Although he also discusses poetry and some of the same themes in another collection, *Art: Yesterday, Today, and Tomorrow,* the talks in *Sufi Poetry* deal far more specifically with symbolism in Persian Sufi poetry and also give us a more detailed presentation of the works of the most famous Persian Sufi poets: Farid ad-Din Attar, Jalal ad-Din Rumi, Muslih ad-Din Sa'di, and Shams ad-Din Muhammad Hafiz.

This edition of *Sufi Poetry* has been carefully re-edited and adapted from the original publication (found in the influential "Sufi Message Series") for clarity in modern English. It has also been made gender inclusive to prevent distortion of the original Message of Hazrat Inayat Khan. Although it was the convention in his own day to use the masculine personal pronoun in an inclusive sense, such use of patriarchal language is no longer considered representative of our current values and is sometimes off-putting to those who might otherwise be inspired by the beautiful and original teachings of the master. Nevertheless, it should be remembered that an adaptation like this one is necessarily an interpretation and liable to error. For this, I take full responsibility. Please know that I have approached the material with the utmost respect and have only made changes in the hope that the updated language and gender inclusivity would help to spread the Message of God "far and wide."

Pir Netanel Mu'in ad-Din, Boulder, Colorado, dedicated to my Sabiha, on January 2nd, 2015, the birthday of Noor Inayat-Khan, and the day on which we read . . .

All names and forms
are garments and covers
under which the one life is hidden.

Sufi Poetry

Prophecy and Persian Sufi Poetry

THE POET AND THE PROPHET

THERE IS A SAYING, "a poet is a prophet." This is a saying of great significance and hidden meaning. There is no doubt that although poetry is not necessarily prophecy, prophecy is born in poetry. Poetry is a body adopted by the spirit of prophecy. Wagner says that noise is not necessarily music; the same can be said of poetry. A verse written in rhyme and meter is not necessarily true poetry. Poetry is an art, a music expressed in the beauty and harmony of words. Of course, much of the poetry one reads is written for amusement or recreation; but real poetry comes from the dancing of the soul. No one can make the soul dance unless the soul itself is inclined to dance. Likewise, no soul can dance which is not alive.

In the Bible, we are taught that no one will "enter the kingdom of God" whose soul has not been "born again."[1] Being "born again" refers to being alive. A cheerful disposition, or an external inclination to merriment, are not the only signs of a living soul.

---

1 *The New Testament,* John 3:3, says: "Truly, truly, no one will see the kingdom of God unless they be born again." And John 3:5, says: "Truly, I tell you, no one can enter the kingdom of God unless they are born of water and the Spirit." Likewise, 1 Peter 1:22-23, says: "Being born again, not of corruptible seed, but of incorruptible, by the word of God, which lives and abides for ever."

External joy and amusement may simply come through the external being of a person. However, even in this outer joy and happiness, there is sometimes a glimpse of inner joy and happiness, which is a sign of the soul having been "born again."

What brings the soul to life? It is brought to life when it touches its own depths. When the soul comes up against the iron wall of this life of falsehood, and instead of reaching outward, turns within, it encounters itself and begins to come to life. Our nature is such that when we meet with obstacles, we struggle with them. For the sensitive person, the person with a sympathetic and tender heart, these obstacles and blows from the outer world make an impact within; and instead of making them want to hit back externally, it only makes them want to go deeper within; for the soul is awakened by the blows of life. This person might have appeared to be living before, but in reality, they were as if dead. But once the soul is awakened, it begins to expresses itself through music, art, poetry, or deeds. This is how the poet is born.

There are two signs which reveal the poet: one is imagination; the other is feeling. Both are essential on the spiritual path. A person who lacks these qualities, however learned and good, can never arrive at a satisfactory place on the spiritual path. The scriptures of all peoples and ages—whether those of the Hindus, the Parsis, or the Children of Israel *(beni Israel)*— were all given in poetry or poetic prose. No spiritual person, however great or spiritually advanced, has ever been able to give a scripture to the world unless blessed with the gift of poetry. One wonders if this is still possible today, when more refined sentiments are little appreciated and people wish everything to be expressed plainly, 'cut-and-dry,' as the saying goes. People have become accustomed to having everything explained in almost scientific terms. The facts concerning the 'names and forms' of this world may be explained scientifically, in colorless words; but when one wishes to interpret the sensations aroused by actually looking at life, it cannot be done except in the way the prophets did it in poetry. No one has ever explained, nor can anyone ever explain the truth in words, least of all in ordinary language. Most language exists for the convenience of everyday affairs. The deepest sentiments cannot be explained in this language. The message that the prophets have given to the world at different times is an interpretation of life as they have received it.

Inspiration begins in poetry and culminates in prophecy. The poet is a soul who has, as it were, risen from the grave and begun to move gracefully. When that soul begins to dance, moving beautifully in all directions between heaven and earth, expressing all the beauty it sees, that is prophecy. When developed, the poet reads the mind of the universe; although often, the poet does not know the actual meaning of what has been said. Often, it is only after many years that one realizes the real meaning. Behind all our activities, the divine spirit is hidden, and often manifests without our realizing it is divine.

In the East, the prophet is called *paighambar,* which

means, 'the messenger,' someone who carries a word to someone else. In reality, everyone in this world is the vehicle of a hidden impulse, and usually without knowing it. This is true of living beings as well as objects. Every object has its purpose; and by fulfilling its purpose, it fulfills the plan of nature. Therefore, whatever a person's activity might be—whether business, science, music, art, or poetry—they are in some way a vehicle. There are vehicles of living beings, and vehicles of those who have passed to the other side; vehicles who represent their country, and vehicles who represent their people. Everyone is acting in their own way as a vehicle.

When the prophet or poet dives deeply within, they touch that perfection which is the source and goal of all beings. As an electric wire connected with a battery receives the force or energy of the battery, so the poet who has touched the inmost depths of their being has touched the divine perfection. From there, they derive that wisdom, that beauty, and that power which belong to the perfect Self of God.

In all things, there is both the real and the false, the raw and the ripe. Poetry comes from the tendency to contemplation. A person with imagination cannot retain the imagination, cannot mold it, cannot build it up, unless they have this contemplative tendency within. The more time one spends in contemplation, the more one is able to conceive of what one receives. After contemplation, a person is able to realize an idea more clearly than if that idea had merely passed through the mind.

The process of contemplation is like the workings of a camera. When the camera is put before an object and properly focused, the image of that object is received by the camera. Likewise, when one focuses on an object, one can see that object more clearly. The appeal of poets is that they can tell their readers of things they have seen behind what is generally recognized. But the prophet goes still further, being able to contemplate any idea with the same focus. There comes a time in the life of the prophet, or of any contemplative, when whatever object they cast their glance upon opens up and reveals its heart. In the history of the world, we see that the prophets—aside from their great imaginations, their great dreams, ecstasy and joy in the divine life—have also been great reformers, scientists, doctors, or even diplomats. This in itself shows their balance. They are not merely dreamers who go into trances; both sides of their personality are equally developed.

It is the divinity of the human being that the prophets manifest. We can see this in the life of Joseph. We are told that he was so innocent that he went with his brothers, yielding to them, and that this led to his betrayal. In his relationship with Zulaikha, we see the human being, the tendency to beauty. At the same time, he continually asks, "What am I doing? What shall I do?" Later in his life, we see him as one who knows the secret of dreams, as the mystic who interprets the dream of Pharaoh. Still later, we see that be became a minister, with the administration of the country in his hands, carrying-out the work of the state.[2]

Spirituality has become too far removed from material life, and thus, God has become far removed from humanity. Therefore, people can no longer conceive of God as speaking through a human being, through someone like yourself. Even the religious who read the Bible every day will have great difficulty in understanding the verse, "Be you perfect, even as your Father in heaven is perfect."[3] The Sufi message and its mission are to bring this truth to the consciousness of the world: that the human being can dive so deep within so as to touch the depths where one is united with the whole of life, with all souls, and there derive from that source, harmony, beauty, peace, and power.

---

2 Parallel Joseph narratives are found in the Torah in the book of Genesis, chapters 37-50, and in the Qur'an, in chapters 6, 12, and 40.
3 *The New Testament*, Matthew 5:48.

THE IMAGERY OF SUFI POETRY

THE IMAGERY OF Sufi poetry stands apart, being distinct and peculiar in character. It is both admired and criticized for its peculiarity. It is different in expression from the poetry of other lands because of its Persian origins and the particular qualities of Persia. These qualities include its fine climate and ancient traditions. It is said to be the place where wine was tasted for the first time. It is a land of luxury, beauty, art, and imagination. It was natural then that Persian thinkers of all periods, thinking deeply about life, about its nature and character, should become subtle and artistic in their expression. In short, it is the dancing of the soul at work. In most people, the soul is asleep; but when the soul has awakened, called by beauty, it leaps up to dance. Then its every movement makes a picture, whether in prose, poetry, music, or another expression. A dancing soul will always express the most subtle and intricate harmonies in the realm of music or poetry.

When we read the works of Hafiz and many other Sufi poets, we find they are full of the same imagery. In part, this is due to the Islamic environment. Islam has a particular object in view, and in order to attain that object, has strict rules about life. In that environment, liberal thinkers often had difficulty expressing themselves without being accused of doing a great harm to religion and the state. Nevertheless, the liberal thinkers of Persia, with their dancing souls and continual enthusiasm, began to express their souls in a very particular imagery, speaking of 'the beloved,' 'wine,' the 'wine-press,' and 'the tavern.' This poetry became so popular that both the wise and the simple benefited, the latter enjoying the beauty of its wonderful expressions, which were immediately appealing to every soul. Souls already awakened, and those on the point of awakening, were inspired by these poems. Souls who were opening their eyes after a deep slumber of many years began to rise up and dance. As Hafiz said, "If the pious in long robes listen to my verse, my song, they will immediately get up and dance." At the end of the poem, he writes, "Please forgive me, pious ones, for I am drunk!"

The imagery of drinking is used to convey many different meanings. Imagine a magic tavern with many different wines. Each vintage has a different effect upon the person who drinks it. One drinks a wine that makes them light-hearted, frivolous, humorous. Another drinks a wine that makes them sympathetic, kind, tender, and gentle. Someone else drinks one that makes them bewildered at everything they see. Another drinks and finds a way into the ditch. One becomes angry after drinking, while another becomes passionate. One drinks and is drowned in despair. Another drinks and begins to feel loving and affectionate. Yet another drinks a wine that makes them discouraged with everything. Imagine how interested we should all be to see that tavern! Well, we live in that tavern and see it every day; only we do not take proper notice of it.

Once I saw a *majdhūb* (a man pretending to be insane, who, although living *in the world* did not wish to be *of the world)* standing on the street of a large city, laughing. I stood there, curious to know what made him laugh at that moment. Finally I saw it was the sight of so many drunken people, each one having had their particular vintage.

It really is amusing when we look at it in this way. There is not a single person on earth who does not drink, but the wine of one is different from the wine of another. A person drinks all day and all night, always waking in the morning intoxicated by whatever vintage he or she has been drinking, waking with fear or anger, joy, love, or affection.

Why did the great Sufi teachers take such an interest in the imagery of these poets? They found the solution to the problem of life by looking upon the world as a tavern with many wines, each person drinking a different vintage. They discovered the alchemy, the chemical process, by which to change one vintage of wine into another. The work of the Sufi teacher is to find out which kind wine the *murīd* is currently drinking, and exchange it for the kind the *murīd* needs to drink.

Is there then no place for soberness in life? There is, but when that soberness is properly interpreted, one sees that it too is a kind of intoxication from a particular vintage of wine. Amir, the Hindustani poet, has expressed it in verse: "The eyes of the sober one spoke to the eyes of the drunken one, 'You have no place here, for your intoxication is different from mine.' " The awakened person seems to be asleep to the sleeping one, and so the one who has become sober also appears to be still drunk. The condition of life is such that no one appears to be sober. It is this soberness that is called *nirvāna* by Buddhists and *mūktī* by Hindus. If I were asked if it is then desirable for us to be sober, my reply would be, "No." What is desirable is for us to know what soberness is; and after knowing what soberness is, to then take any wine we may choose. The tavern is there, the wines are there.

There are two kinds of people: those who are masters of wine, and those who are slaves to wine. One drinks the wine, but the other, the wine drinks until empty. The one whom wine drinks is mortal; but the one who drinks the wine becomes immortal. What is the love of God? What is divine knowledge? Is it not a wine? Its experience is different, its intoxication is different, for there is ordinary wine and there is expensive champagne. The difference is in the wine.

In the imagery of the Sufi poets, the tavern is the world, and the *sāqī*, the 'wine-bearer,' is God. In whatever form the wine-bearer comes, it is God. In this way, recognizing the *sāqī*, the wine-bearer, in all forms, the Sufi worships God. We recognize God in friend and foe as the wine-bearer. Wine is the influence that we receive from life—a harmonious influence or a depressing influence, a beautiful influence or one that lacks beauty. When we have given in to it, then we become drunk, then we become addicted to it, then we are under its influence. However, when we have sought soberness, then we have risen above it, and all wines are ours.

THE PERSIAN POETS

PERSIA HAS ALWAYS had great poets, and has even been called, "The Land of Poetry." This is because the Persian (Farsi) language is so well adapted to poetry, and also because all Persian poetry contains a mystical touch. Its quality and composition make it poetry; but its mysticism makes it prophecy.

The climate and atmosphere of Persia, as well as the imaginative nature of the people, have made the poetry rich. When the imagination has no scope for expansion, then poetry dies, and materialism increases.

There is no poet in the world who is not a mystic. A poet is a mystic, whether consciously or unconsciously; for no one can write poetry without inspiration. When a poet touches the profound depths of the spirit, struck by some aspect of life, they bring forth a poem, as a diver brings forth a pearl.

In this age of materialism and ever-growing commercialism, humanity seems to have lost the way of inspiration. During my travels, I was asked by a well-known writer whether it is really true that there is such a thing as 'inspiration.' This gave me an inkling as to just how far some writers and poets are removed from inspiration today. It is the materialism of the age that is responsible for this. If a person has a predisposition to poetry or music today, then as soon as they begin writing, their first thought is, *Will it catch on, or not? What is its practical value?* Generally, what 'catches on' is that which appeals to the average person. In this way, culture is diminished instead of elevated.

When the soul of the poet is intoxicated by the beauty of nature and the harmony of life, it is moved to dance, and the expression of that dance is poetry. The difference between inspired poetry and simple mechanical writing is as great as the difference between true and false. Over the centuries, generations of Persian poets have created a wonderful treasure of thought for humanity. Jalal ad-Din Rumi has revealed in his *Masnavī* the profound mystery of revelation. In the East, his works are considered as sacred as scripture. They have illuminated countless souls, and their study fulfills the highest standards of culture.

The poet is a creator, and creates in spite of all obstacles. Poets create a world of their own; and in so doing, rise above the notion that only what is visible or tangible is regarded as real. When they sing to the sun, when they smile at the moon, when they pray to the sea and gaze at the plants, the forests, and at life in the desert, they communicate with nature. To the eyes of the ordinary person, the poet is imaginative, a dreamer, and a visionary, whose thoughts seem to be floating in the air. But if one asks a poet about those who see them this way, he or she will say that it is those who cannot fly who remain on the ground. It is natural that the creatures who walk on the earth are not always able to fly. Those who fly must have wings. Among human beings, one finds the same difference, for in human beings are all things. There are souls like those of germs or worms, there are souls like those of four-legged animals or birds, and there are souls like those of *jinn* and angels. Among human beings, all can be found—those which belong to the earth, those who dwell in heaven, and those which dwell in the depths.

Those who were able to soar by the power of their imagination were 'living poets.' What they said was not merely a statement; it was music itself. It had rhythm and tone. It made their souls dance, and anyone who heard it also wished to dance. Thus, Hafiz of Shiraz challenged the dignified and pious of his country, saying, "Pious friends, you would forget your dignity if you would hear the song that came from my glowing heart." It is such souls, touching the highest summits of life, that have been able to contribute some truth to us, giving us an interpretation of human nature and the inner law of life.

Poets who make poetry for the sake of 'name and fame,' to be popular or appreciated by others, are another thing entirely. That is business, not poetry. Poetry is an art of the highest degree. The poet's communication with nature, in the end, leads to a deeper communication within. By that communication, the poet delves deeper within and without, ultimately communicating with life everywhere. This communication brings one into a state of ecstasy; and in that ecstasy, one's whole being is filled with joy. The poet forgets the worries and anxieties of life, rising above the 'praise and blame' of this world, its objects diminishing in importance. The poet stands on the earth, but gazes into the heavens, their outlook on life broadened and their sight more keen. They see things that no one else is interested in, that no one can see.

This teaches us that what may be called 'heaven' or 'paradise,' is not very far from us. It is always near, if we will only look for it. Our life is what we examine. If we examine it in the right light, then it is right. If we examine it the wrong light, then it is wrong. Our life is made according to our own attitude, and that is why the poet proves self-sufficient, as well as indifferent and independent. These qualities become wings allowing the poet to soar. The poet is in the same position as anyone else with regard to the fears and worries of life, the troubles and difficulties that everyone feels in the midst of the world. Yet, the poet rises above these things.

No doubt, poets are more sensitive to the troubles and difficulties of life than ordinary people. If they really took to heart everything that came to them, all the jarring influences that disturb one's peace of mind, all the sharp and abrasive edges of life that scrape us all, then they would not be able to go on. On the other hand, if they harden their hearts and make them less sensitive, then they would also be closing their hearts to the inspiration which comes as poetry. Therefore, in order to open the doors of the heart, to keep its sensitivity, the poet who communicates with life, both within and without, is open to all influences, whether agreeable or disagreeable, and is without protection; the only escape is to rise above them.

The prophetic message given by Zarathustra to the people of Persia was poetic from beginning to end. It is interesting that Zarathustra demonstrates in his scriptures, and through his life, how a poet rises from earth to heaven. Zarathustra communicated with nature, with its beauty, and with every step touched deeper and deeper into the depths of life. Zarathustra formed his religion by praising the beauty in nature, and by finding the source of his art, which is creation itself, in the Divine Artist behind it all.

What form of worship did he teach? He taught the same worship with which he began his poetry, and with which he finished it. He said to his pupils: "Stand before the sea; look at its vastness; bow before it, before its source and goal." He said to them: "Look at the sun, and see what joy it brings. What is behind it? Where does it come from? Think of its source and goal, and how you are heading toward it." People thought that this was sun worship, but it was not; it was the worship of Light, which is the source and goal of all. That communication within and without sometimes extended the range of a poet's vision, so much so that it was beyond the comprehension of the average person.

When the Shah of Persia said that he would like to have the history of his country written, for one did not exist at that time, Firdausi, an inspired and intuitive poet responded, "I will write it and bring it to you."

He began to meditate, throwing his search-light as far back into the past as possible; and before the appointed time, he was able to prepare that book and bring it to the court. It is said that the spiritual power of that poet was so great that when someone at the court sneered at the idea of a man being able to look so far back into the past, he went up to him and put his hand on his forehead and said, "Now, see!" And the man saw with his own eyes that which was written in the book!

This is human, not superhuman, although examples of it are found but rarely. For in the life of every human being, especially of one who is pure-hearted, loving, sympathetic, and good, the past, present, and future are manifested to a certain extent. If one's inner light is turned to the past like a search-light, it can go much further than we can comprehend. Some have to develop this gift, while others are born with it. Among those who are born with it, we find some who, perhaps, know ten or twelve years beforehand what is going to happen. Therefore, a poet is someone who can sometimes focus the soul on the past and also throw light on the future. They make clear that which has not yet happened, but which has been planned beforehand, and which already exists in the abstract.

It is such poetry that becomes inspirational poetry. It is through this poetry that the intricate aspects of metaphysics are taught. The Vedas and the Upanishads are all written in poetry. The surahs of the Qur'an and Zarathustra's scriptures are all in poetry. All of these prophets brought the message in poetry.

The development of poetry in Persia occurred at a time when there was a great conflict between the orthodox and liberal thinkers. At that time, the law of Persia was a religious law, and no one was at liberty to express thoughts which might be in conflict with religious ideas. There were great thinkers—such as Firdausi, Farid ad-Din Attar, Jalal ad-Din Rumi, Sa'di, Hafiz, Jami, and Omar Khayyam—who were not only poets, but poetry itself. They were living in another world, though they appeared on earth. Their outlook on life, their keen insight, was different from that of everyone else. The words which arose in their hearts were not brought forth with effort, but were natural flames of the burning heart. And these words remain as flames enlightening the souls of all times.

Sufism has been the wisdom of these poets. There has never been a poet of note in Persia who was not a Sufi, and every one of them added something to Sufi ideas. However, they took great care not to affront the minds of the orthodox entirely and spoke symbolically. Therefore, a new terminology had to be invented in Persian poetry. The poets spoke of 'the beloved' and 'the rose,' words which would not offend the orthodox mind, and yet, at the same time, would serve as symbolic expressions of divinity.

It is the work of Sufism today to interpret the ideas of these poets, to express their ideas in words that can be understood by modern people; for the value of those ideas is as great today as it ever was.

FARID AD-DIN ATTAR

FARID AD-DIN ATTAR was one of the earliest Sufi poets of Persia, and there is no doubt that the work of Attar was the inspiration of Rumi and many other spiritual souls and poets of Persia. He showed the way to the ultimate aim of life by making a sort of picture in poetic form. Almost all the great teachers of the world, when pointing the way for other seeking souls, have had to adopt symbolic forms of expression, such as stories or legends, which give a key to those who are ready to understand, and yet, still interest those who are not. Thus, both the sleepers and the already awakened may rejoice in them. This method was followed by the poets of Persia and India, especially the Hindustani poets. They have told their stories in a form that would be acceptable, not only to the seekers after truth, but also to those of all stages of evolution.

Attar's best known work is *Mantiq-ut-Tair*, or the 'Conference of the Birds,' from which the idea of the Blue Bird has been taken. Very few have understood the idea of the Blue Bird, or the Bird of the Sky. It contains a very ancient teaching through the use of the Persian word for sky. This teaching points out that every soul has a capacity which may be called the 'sky,' a capacity that can accommodate either earth or heaven, whichever it partakes of and holds within itself. When one walks in a crowd, what does one see? One sees faces; but one might better call them attitudes. All that we see, all that presents itself to us, has expression, atmosphere, and form. If we were to give it a name, it would be 'attitude.' Whatever attitude they have to life, whether right or wrong, good or bad, they are themselves that attitude. This is the idea of the 'sky' in Persian.

Whatever attitude one takes, one embodies that attitude, or becomes that attitude. The source of happiness or unhappiness is really within us. When we are unaware of this, we cannot get our lives together; but as we become more acquainted with this secret, we actually gain mastery over our lives. This process of discovery and attainment of mastery is the purpose of this life. And it is this process which is explained by Attar in his description of the seven valleys through which this Bird of the Sky has passed.

THE SEVEN VALLEYS

The first valley is the Valley of the Quest. Every child is born with the tendency to search and to know. What we call 'inquisitiveness' or 'curiosity,' is something born within each of us, and represents the inner quest. As we are born with this tendency, we cannot be satisfied until we have obtained the knowledge we wish to have. But there is also no doubt that what truly prevents us from gaining that knowledge for which the soul is actually searching is us. It is the smaller self, or the false self that is always standing in the way, and which keeps us from searching for the one thing that every soul struggles to find. Therefore, it is safe to say, we have no enemy more dangerous to our happiness than ourselves.

Some people use science or art to reach the end of this quest, to discover what is behind this manifestation. Whether one is exploring the material or the spiritual, in the end, one will and must arrive at the ultimate goal, which is the same for everyone. Even scientists and engineers, people who are absorbed in research into material things and hardly ever think of spiritual matters, will, after much searching, arrive at something very close to the ultimate knowledge. Therefore, whatever a person may seem to us—materialist, atheist, or agnostic—we cannot really call them that, because in the end, their goal and attainment is the same. If one reaches the depths of knowledge, if one goes far enough, then—no matter what it was for which they were originally searching—they will arrive at the common goal.

When we have searched long enough and found something satisfying, we still cannot enjoy it unless one faculty is operative—the faculty of love and devotion. Do we not see in our lives everyday, that even people of great intellect and accomplishment are often still missing something? Among couples, when one is overly intellectual, does not the other feel that something is lacking in their relationship? That it is missing the heart? The heart adds balance to life, and its absence creates a wasteland. Knowledge and heart are like two forces that keep life in balance. If the heart-quality is especially strong and the intellect is lacking, then life also lacks balance. Knowledge and heart must be developed together. Therefore, according to Attar, the faculty of devotion or heart is the Second Valley, the Valley of Love.

The Third Valley is the Valley of Knowledge, the knowledge that illuminates us and arises with the help of love and the intellect. This is spiritual knowledge. Without a well-developed love-quality, we are incapable of acquiring such knowledge. There are nuances in one's life that cannot be perceived and fully understood without having touched the depths of life, which are devotional. A person who has never been grateful, who has never been in the position of feeling grateful, cannot know gratitude or receive it. One who has not experienced humility, does not know its beauty. The one who has not known gentleness or modesty, cannot appreciate its loveliness or recognize it.

A person of refined qualities is often ridiculed if they happen to be in a place where their qualities are not understood, where they are received like a foreign language. This shows us that there is a refinement in life for which intellect alone is not sufficient. The heart must be open too. A very intellectual man once went to Jami and asked him to take him as his pupil, to give him an initiation. Jami looked at him and said, "Have you ever loved anyone?" The man said, "No, I have not loved." Then Jami said, "Go and love first; then come back to me and I will show you the way."

Love has a part to play at every stage of life. As a child, as a youth, as an adult—whatever stage of life one has reached—love is always asked for, and always has its part to play. Whatever the situation in which we are placed—among friends or foes, among those who understand us or those who do not, in ease or difficulty, in all places at all times—love has its part to perform. People who think, "I must not let love have its way; I must harden myself against it," only imprison their souls. There is only one thing in this world that shows us the true sign of heaven, that gives us actual proof of the divine, and that is pure, unselfish love.

All the noble qualities hidden in the soul spring forth and blossom when love helps and nurtures them. We may have a great deal of good in us, and we may be very intelligent, but as long as our hearts are closed, we cannot demonstrate true nobility, that goodness which is hidden in our hearts. The psychology of the heart is such that, once one begins to know it, one realizes that life is an ever-unfolding phenomenon. Every moment becomes a miracle; a search-light is thrown on human nature, and all things become so clear that one does not ask for any greater phenomenon or miracle; it is a miracle in itself. What people call telepathy, mind-reading, or clairvoyance, and other such things, these come by themselves when the heart is open.

When people are cold or rigid, inside they feel as if they are already dead. They are not living; they cannot enjoy life, for they cannot express themselves and cannot see the light and life outside. What keeps us from developing the heart? Our exacting attitude. We want to make a transaction out of love. We say, "If you will love me, I will love you." As soon as we begin to measure and weigh our favors, our service, and all that we do for the beloved, we cease to know what love is. Love sees the beloved . . . and nothing else.

As Rumi says, "Whether you love a human being or God, there will come a day when all lovers, either of human beings or God, will be brought before the throne of love, and the presence of the only Beloved will reign there." What does this show us? In loving our friend, our neighbor, or even an enemy, one is only loving God. The person who says, "I love You, God, but I cannot love a human being," does not even love God. It is like saying, "I love you very much, but I don't like your face!"

After this Third Valley, where the knowledge of human nature and more refined feelings called 'virtues' are attained, the next step is Annihilation. What we tend to call destruction or annihilation is nothing but change. Neither substance nor form nor spirit is ever absolutely destroyed; it is only changed. Nevertheless, we often resist change. We have difficulty with it and don't like it, but we cannot live without it either. There is not a single moment of life without change. Whether we accept it or not, change is happening. Destruction, annihilation, or death might seem like a significant change; yet, we die a thousand deaths in lifetime. Great disappointments, and moments when our hearts break, are worse than death. Often our experiences of life are worse than death, yet we go through them. At the time, they seem unbearable; we think we cannot stand them, and yet we go on living. If we are still living after dying a thousand such deaths, then there is nothing left in the world of which to be afraid. It is our delusion, our own imagination, which makes death so dreadful to us. Can anyone kill life? If there is any death, it is that of death itself, for life will not die.

Someone once went to a Sufi with a question. He said, "I have been puzzling over something for many years, reading many books, and I still have not been able to find a satisfactory answer to this question. Tell me, what happens after death?" The Sufi replied, "You should ask this of someone who is going to die; I am going to live." Again, the idea is that of the 'sky,' a capacity that can accommodate different things. Sometimes when we use the word, 'accommodation,' we mean a room. And what has taken possession of this accommodation, the room of our being? A deluded ego that says, 'I.' It is deluded by this body and mind and has called itself 'an individual.' When a person has a ragged coat, they say, 'I am poor,' when in reality it is the coat that is poor. What this accommodation or capacity contains is that which becomes our knowledge, our realization, and it is that which limits us. It forms that limitation which is the tragedy of every soul.

Now, this capacity may be filled with self, or it may be filled with God. There is only room for one. Either we live with our limitation, or we let God reign there in unlimited Being. In other words, we take away the home which has always belonged to God and occupy it with delusion, calling it our own. Not only do we call it our own, but we even call it our 'self.' That is our delusion, and all religious and philosophical teachings are given in order to rid us of this delusion that deprives us of spiritual wealth. Spiritual wealth is the greatest wealth. Spiritual happiness is the only happiness; there is no other.

Once we have disillusioned ourselves, we arrive at the Fourth Valley, the Valley of Non-Attachment, and here we are afraid. We think: 'How can I give my home to someone else, even if it is God? This is *my* body, *my* mind, *my* home, *my* individuality. How can I give it away, even to God?' But, in reality, these attachments are not things upon which we can rely. They are delusion from beginning to end and subject to destruction. Does anything stand above destruction? Nothing. So why be afraid? This fear is natural, and arises because we are unaccustomed to facing reality. We are so used to fantasies that we are actually afraid of reality. We are afraid of losing ourselves; but non-attachment is not losing one's self, it is the loss of illusion. In reality, it is only by losing the illusion that we can find ourselves. Our souls are lost in this illusion, and we need to get out of it, to rise above it.

By the time we reach the Fifth Valley, the Valley of Unity, we have disillusioned ourselves about attachment; and it is this act which is called being 'born again' in the New Testament.[4] When the soul emerges from illusion, it is being born. How does the birth of the soul express itself? What does one feel? It expresses itself first in a kind of wonder and great

---

4 *The New Testament,* John 3:3.

joy. A person's interest in life is increased; everything one sees brings enjoyment. One is concerned with little, but wonders at everything. The wonder is such that it becomes tremendously amusing to look at life. The whole world becomes a stage full of players. One begins to play along with the people of this world, as one might play along with the games of children, and yet, not being much concerned with what they do, for one expects nothing different from them. When children play their games, their parents are not much concerned about them. They know it's a stage in the child's life and they cannot expect anything different from them. So, likes and dislikes, may interest one at this stage, but they will not affect one in the least.

There is another stage, where this wonder allows a person to see the reflection of the One who has taken possession of the heart. One sees the Beloved in everyone, even in one's enemy. The Beloved is seen in all things, and thus, the 'bowl of poison' given by the Beloved is not so bitter. Those who, like Christ, have sacrificed themselves and suffered for humanity, have revealed a God-consciousness which has reached the stage where even one's enemy appears to be the Friend, the Beloved. It is not an unattainable stage, for the soul is made of love, and is continually evolving toward the perfection of love. All the virtues we have learned as human beings, love has taught us. Therefore, this world of good and bad, of thorns and flowers, can truly become a place of unending splendor.

In the Sixth Valley, the Valley of Amazement, a person recognizes and understands what is beyond all things, the reason of all reasons, the cause of all causes; for all intuition and power develop in a person at this stage of unfoldment.

The Seventh Valley, the Valley of God-Realization, is the valley of that peace for which every soul searches, whether spiritually or materially, seeking from morning until night for something that will give it peace. To some souls, that peace comes when one is asleep; but for the God-conscious, that peace becomes one's home. As soon as one closes one's eyes, as soon as one relaxed one's body, stilling the mind and losing the limitations of consciousness, one begins to float in the unlimited spheres.

JALAL AD-DIN RUMI

THE POETRY OF Jalal ad-Din Rumi has made a great impression upon humanity. In the beginning, he was inspired by Farid ad-Din Attar. Although Rumi was a highly educated man with the gift of speech, his soul did not achieve enlightenment until he met Shams-i Tabriz, a wandering dervish, later in life. The latter came to him dressed in rags, showing no exceptional learning which would be prized by the world; and yet, he was in tune with the infinite and, to speak in religious terms, had gained the "kingdom of Heaven."

This apparent beggar came to the home of Rumi, who welcomed him, as was his custom. Rumi was then working on a manuscript, and the first thing Shams-i Tabriz did was grab the manuscript and throw it away. Rumi looked at him in wonder. But Shams-i Tabriz said, "Haven't you had enough of reading and the study of books yet? Study life instead!" Rumi listened respectfully as he continued, "All these things which seem so important to you, what are they on the day you die? What is rank? What is position? What is power? A far greater question is—what will go with you? The answer to that question will lead you to eternity. The problems of this world, you can solve and go on solving, but they never end. What have you really

SUFI POETRY: PROPHECY AND PERSIAN SUFI POETRY

understood about God, about human beings? What relationship have you found between us and God? And if you worship God, do you really know why? What is limitation? What is perfection? And how can one seek it?"

After this conversation, Rumi realized that it is not learning, but living that counts. He must live the knowledge. Up to this point, he had read much, thought much, and talked much, but he suddenly saw that what is truly important is not talking about the truth, but living it and being it. When he realized this— after Shams-i Tabriz had left—he wrote the following verse: "The Sovereign of earth and of heaven, of whom people have spoken, today I have seen in the form of a human being." For he had just seen how profoundly great the heart of human being can be, how deeply the soul can be touched, and how high the spirit can reach.

After this, Rumi immediately set-out after this dervish. His family and his friends were against it, because mystics and dervishes of this type are strange to ordinary people, something not quite of this world. Their language is different, their ways unusual, and their ideas do not correspond with those of practical people. So naturally, they thought Rumi was heading in the wrong direction.

Rumi gave up his teaching position and wandered from place to place with Shams-i Tabriz. During this period, he was much criticized and there were murmurings against Shams-i Tabriz by Rumi's former pupils. After several months, his master Shams-i Tabriz suddenly disappeared one day, leaving Rumi in terrible sorrow. He had given up his position and his way of life, and now the teacher whom he had chosen to follow had abandoned him. But this was an initiation for Rumi, the birth of his soul. From that moment on, he looked at life from a very different perspective.

For a long time after, Jalal ad-Din Rumi lived in an ecstatic state, during which he wrote the *Dīvān of Shams-i Tabriz*. Because of the union he had achieved with the heart of his teacher, he began to see all of which his teacher had thought and spoken. For this reason, he did not consider it his book, but his teacher's book. His heart, which had listened so attentively to the master, had become a faithful recorder. All that had been spoken by Shams-i Tabriz began to repeat itself in Rumi, and he experienced a wonderful fulfillment, a great joy and exaltation. Soon, Rumi began to write verses, which musicians began to take up and sing. When Rumi heard these beautiful verses sung by the musicians, accompanied by the *rebab*, a Persian musical instrument, he experienced *wajd* or 'ecstasy,' what is called *samadhi* by the yogis.

People have become so materially oriented today that they are afraid of experiences beyond those of the ordinary senses. They only believe in that which can be experienced through these senses. That which is goes beyond these is something of which one should be afraid; those are deep waters, unnatural, or at least unexplored territory. Often, people are afraid of falling into trances, or of having strange experiences that stimulate unusual feelings, thinking that those who experience such things are fanatics who have gone out of their minds. It is not so. Thought belongs to the mind, feeling to the heart. Why should one believe that thought is right and feeling is wrong?

All the different meditation experiences are of thought and feeling; but the poet who receives inspiration experiences a joy that others cannot experience. It is a joy that belongs to inspiration and the poet knows it. The composer, after having written a new piece of music, is filled with a certain joy, a certain fulfillment that others do not know.

Do poets or musicians lose their minds in composing their works? On the contrary, they become more complete. They experience a wider, deeper, keener, more fulfilling life than others live. A life of sensation lacks the experience of exaltation. Even religious prayers, rituals and ceremonies were intended to produce exaltation; for it is one of the needs of life. Exaltation is as necessary, or perhaps more necessary, than the cultivation of thought.

Rumi had many disciples who came to him for guidance. Through his deep sorrow and bewilderment over the loss of Shams-i Tabriz, he achieved another outlook entirely; his vision became different. Thus, he came to write his most valuable work, which is studied in all the countries of the East: It is called *Masnavi-i Ma'navi*. It is a living scripture which has enlightened numerous souls. It is simplicity itself, and yet, has led sincere seekers into the deepest depths. There is no complexity in it, no dogmas, no principles, no great moral teachings, no expressions of piety. It is the Law of Life expressed in a kind of word-picture.

In this work, Rumi tries to explain the meaning of the prophetic mission in verse through his mystic vision. In the Western world, many people have never even thought about prophecy or the work of the prophet in the world. What they know of prophets is usually confined to what they know of the Hebrew Bible and, if they are Christians, they are often seen as preparing the world for the message of Jesus Christ. But what Rumi wished to explain about prophethood was the meaning of Jesus' words, "I am the Alpha and the Omega."[5] Rumi wanted to say that the One who is first and last, was, is, and ever shall be, and that we should not limit that One to a single period in history.

Then Rumi explains that the words of the prophet are the words of God. He uses the example the reed flute, which is open at one end, while the other end is in the mouth of the musician. The prophet is the flute, God the musician, and the sound the Message. Muslims have never called the Message given by the Prophet Muhammad *his* Message; they always speak of *kalām-allāh,* which means, the 'Word of God.' Thus, their religion is not called Muhammadanism, but Islam, or 'peace.' They find it offensive for people to speak of 'Muhammadan religion,' for the Prophet was the instrument through which God expressed the divine Message. God is capable of speaking through any instrument; all and everything are instruments of God. It is the spirit of God which must be brought forward.

Rumi's words are so deep, so perfect, so touching,

5 *The New Testament,* Revelation 21:6.

37

that when one repeats them, hundreds and thousands of others are moved to tears. They cannot help penetrating the heart. This shows how much Rumi himself was moved, to have created such living words. Many wanted to call him a prophet, but he said, "No, I am not a prophet; I am a poet." When Hafiz wrote about Rumi, he said: "I am not capable of writing about the verses of Rumi. What I can say is that he is not a prophet, but he is the one who brought the Sacred Book." In other words, he wanted to say that, in fact, he was a prophet!

No other poet of Persia has given us such a wonderful picture of metaphysics, of the path of evolution and of higher realization, as Rumi, although the form of his poetry is not so beautiful as that of Hafiz. Explaining about the soul, Rumi tells us: "The melodious music that comes as a cry of the heart from the reed flute brings you a message. The flute wants to say, 'I was taken from the reed bed to which I belonged; I was cut from that reed bed, and several holes were made in my heart. And it is this that made me sad, and my cry appeals to every human being.' "

By the flute, he means the soul, the soul which has been cut off from its origins, from the reed bed, which is God. The constant cry of the soul, whether it knows it or not, is to find again that reed bed from which it has been cut off. It is this longing which people who do not understand misinterpret and attribute to lack of wealth or position or failure in worldly ambitions. However, those who understand, find the real meaning of this longing, which is to come nearer to the Source, as the reed longs to find the reed bed.

The difference between Jalal ad-Din Rumi's work and the work of the great Hafiz of Shiraz is that Hafiz has depicted the outer life, whereas Rumi has depicted the inner life. If I were to compare the three greatest poets of Persia, I would call Sa'di the body of the poet, Hafiz the heart of the poet, and Rumi the soul of the poet.

Muslih ad-Din Sa'di

In the East, the works of Sa'di have been considered simple, educational, and at the same time, uplifting. In India, Sa'di's poem *Karima* is taught to children of nine or ten. But this work is not just a legend or an amusing story; it is like a seed sown in the heart of a child, so that, in time, it may flourish and bring forth fruits of good thought and imagination. *Karima* is a poem of thanksgiving. In it, the first lesson Sa'di gives is how to be grateful, how to express gratitude, how to be appreciative. He gives the lesson of gratefulness and appreciation for everything in the world, for the kindness and love of a mother and father, of a friend or companion, by first teaching gratefulness to God for all the blessings and benefits we receive.

Sa'di was a lover of humor and a very simple man. He began his *Gulistan* with a prayer: "Let me not show my infirmities to others; but to You, my Sustainer, You are the Judge, and You are the one who forgives. You choose as You like, whether to be Judge or Forgiver." The way in which he proceeds in this prayer is wonderful and so simple, and yet it has touched thousands and thousands of people.

In *Karima*, Sa'di begins by saying, "Oh Lord, most merciful, I ask Your forgiveness, for I am limited; and in this life of limitation, I am always apt to err." In the first lesson, he teaches that we should recognize our limited condition and realize that this limitedness makes us subject to error. At the same time, he suggests that the innermost desire of every soul is to rise above limitation and keep from error, to seek divine love and ask pardon, and to appreciate all the blessings received in life in order to rise toward the ideal stage of the humanity.

When we look at life today, it seems that this is the very thing lacking. When children grow up without having learned to appreciate, they often cannot understand what their mother has done for them, what their father has done, what their duty is to friends, to their elders, or their teacher. When they grow up without having developed gratefulness, then the ego naturally develops and becomes a menace. A boy who does not appreciate in his childhood all that his mother has done for him cannot learn to be tender and gentle to his wife, for he should have learned this lesson first with his mother.

Everything that arises by nature has to be refined, and in its fulfillment, it must become perfect. From childhood, there is a self-asserting tendency in human beings. In the nature of the child, the 'I' is most pronounced, and of everything he possesses, he says, 'my.' If this is not changed, if the same attitude persists, when that child grows older, they will become hard to others, and this 'I' and 'my' will cause difficulties for all.

All religious, spiritual, and philosophical teaching

leads us toward the development of the personality. There is something in us that is made by nature, but there is also something that we ourselves have to make. We are born human, but we also develop in order to become human. If we remain only as we were born, and the same qualities with which we were born remain undeveloped and unrefined, then we do not fulfill the object of life. With all the great ones come into this world, whom we recognize as saints and sages, masters, teachers and inspired helpers, it is not always the philosophy they taught, the dogmas or religion they gave, that was of the greatest importance. What was most important was their personality, their person. The teachings of Buddha are held in esteem by millions, but greater than his teachings was the life he lived and the wisdom he expressed in his life, for therein lies the fulfillment of his Message.

We are born with a purpose, and that purpose is fulfilled in the refinement of our personality. The unrefined nature of the ego, when developed through life, has an effect like the prick of a thorn. Wherever, whoever, whatever it touches, it causes some harm or disturbance, some destruction. So, when the personalities of human beings are not refined, and they are confronted with temptations, with all the things that attract them, things they like and admire and wish to possess, then they come up against the conflicting activities of life and they rub against everything like a thorn, tearing it to pieces. And what happens? No doubt when thorns rub against thorns, they crush one another and they feel it less; but when thorns rub against flowers, they tear them to pieces.

If we ask individuals from all walks of life what they find difficult in life, they may say they lack wealth or power or position, but mostly their complaint will be that they are in some way or other hurt by others, by a friend, a parent, a child, their life's companion, a neighbor, or a colleague. They are disturbed or troubled and in difficulty from morning till night by the influence of this thorn of life which touches and scratches them. Yet we do not ponder this subject deeply enough. Life is blinding, and it keeps us always busy and engaged in finding fault with others. We do not find the thorn in ourselves; we always see the thorn in other people.

Sa'di has tried in simple language to help us toward the development of our personality, of the flower-like quality, to train our personality which was made to be a flower and not a thorn. He has called his books, *Gulistan*, which means 'flower bed' or 'rose garden,' and Bustan, a 'place of fragrance.' His whole life's work was to explain to us how the heart can be turned into a flower, and that it is made to spread its perfume. If only one can train it and tend it, it will show the delicacy, beauty and fragrance of a flower, and that is the purpose of our life.

There is no mystification in Sa'di's poetry. It is full of wit and intelligence, and at the same time, it is wholly original. The most wonderful thing in the poetry of Sa'di is his humorous turn of mind. He is always ready to look at the comic side of things and to amuse and enjoy himself. How few of us know what true mirth is, humor that is not made vulgar or abused! It shows us the rhythm and tune of the soul. Without humor, life is dull and depressing. Humor is the reflection of that divine life and sun which makes life like a day full of sunshine. And those who reflect divine wisdom and divine joy add to the expression of their thought when they express their ideas with mirth.

One day, Sa'di was sitting in a bookshop where his own books were sold. The bookseller was absent, and someone came in and asked for one of Sa'di's books, not knowing that he was speaking to the poet, himself. Sa'di said, "What do you like about Sa'di's books?" The customer replied, "Oh, he's a funny guy!" Whereupon, Sa'di made him a present of the book. When he wished to pay for it, Sa'di said, "No, I am Sa'di, and when you called me funny, you gave me all the reward I could wish for!"

He wanted life to be joyous. Spirituality does not mean a sad face and deep sighs. No doubt, there are moments when we sympathize with the troubles of others. There are moments that move us to tears, and there are times when we must close our lips. But there are other moments when we can see the joyous side of life and enjoy its beauties. We are not born for depression and unhappiness. Our very being is happiness. Depression is something unnatural. By this, I do not mean to say that sorrow is a sin, or that suffering is always avoidable. We all have to experience both in life in order to accomplish the purpose of life. We cannot always be smiling, and there is no spiritual evolution in ignoring either side of life. As long as one is not bound, it is no sin to stand in the midst of life. We need not go into the forest away from everyone to show our goodness and our virtue. Of what use is our goodness and virtue if we bury ourselves in the forest? It is in the midst of life that we have to develop and express all that is beautiful, perfect and divine to our souls.

In the *Gulistan*, Sa'di expresses a wonderful thought. He says, "Every soul is meant for a certain purpose, and the light of that purpose has been kindled in that soul." It is one short verse, but it is a volume in itself. It suggests to us that this whole universe is like a single symphony, and that all souls are like the notes. Their activities accord with the rhythm of this symphony, and the purpose of their life is to perfect this symphony.

People are often anxious to do a certain thing, and they wait for years and years, unhappy, in despair, for the right moment to come. The soul knows subconsciously that there is a note to be struck, and at the moment when it strikes that note, the soul will be satisfied. Yet the soul does not know what note it is nor when it will be struck.

What is life, and what keeps us living in this world of limitation, this world of continual changes, full of falsehood and full of suffering and trouble? If there is anything in this world that keeps us alive it is hope, the honey of life. There is not one soul in this world who will say, "Now I am satisfied, I have no further desire." In everyone, whatever their position in life, very rich or very poor, full of health or ailing, in all conditions, they are continually yearning and waiting for something to come. We do not know what, but we are waiting for something to come. The real explanation of life is waiting, waiting for something. And what is it that we await? It is the fulfillment of the purpose of life that comes when the soul strikes that note, the note which is meant to be the soul's note. This is what we seek, whether on the outer plane or on the inner plane.

We have not fulfilled our life's purpose until we have struck that note which is our note; the greatest tragedy in life is obscurity of purpose. When our purpose is unclear, we suffer. It is as if we cannot breath, and do not know what to do. This life presents us with things that interest us momentarily, but as soon as we possesses them, we say, "No, this is not it; it is something else." So we go on in illusion, constantly seeking, and yet not knowing what we need. Blessed are those who know their life's purpose, for that is the first step to fulfillment.

How are we to know our life's purpose? Can anyone tell us? No, no one can tell us, for life in its very nature is self-revealing, and it is our own fault if we are not open to that revelation that life offers. It is not the fault of life. We are the children of nature; therefore, our purpose belongs to nature. It is the artificiality of our lives that brings obscurity, which prevents us from receiving that knowledge which is the revelation of our own souls.

If asked how one should proceed, I would advise the study of every object, whether false or true, which holds and attracts us, either outwardly or inwardly. We should not be doubting and suspicious. What Christ taught from morning until night was faith, but the interpretation generally given to this word does not make it clear. People have said that it means faith in a priest, or a church, or a sect; but that is not the meaning. The true meaning of faith is trust in oneself.

The works of Sa'di, from beginning to end, teach the first lesson of faith, which is to understand that we are not here in this world in vain to waste our lives. We are here for a purpose, everyone for a particular purpose. Each one of us is an atom of the universe, and each of us helps to complete the great symphony; and when we do not strike our unique note, it means that note is lacking in the symphony of the whole. When we do not fulfill our life's purpose in the way for which we were created, we are not living rightly and consequently, we are not happy.

Our happiness depends on living rightly, and right living depends on striking our note. The realization of that purpose is in the book of our heart. Open that book and look at it. The aim of all meditation, concentration, and contemplation, is only to open this book, to focus our mind, and to see what purpose there is in our life. As soon as we see that, our ultimate goal, our life's object and happiness, our true health and well-being, and our real wealth lie in the fulfillment of our purpose, then the whole trend of our life will change.

SHAMS AD-DIN MUHAMMAD HAFIZ

THE NAME OF Hafiz is well known to everyone interested in the poetry of Persia because among the Persian poets, Hafiz is unique in his depth of thought and the excellence of the symbolism with which he expresses his thoughts and philosophical ideas.

There was a time when a deep and independent thinker had great difficulty in expressing their thoughts. Although this has not entirely changed, there does seem, in some ways, to be much more freedom of expression today. In times past, when anyone expressed their thoughts freely about life and its hidden law, about the soul, God, creation and manifestation, they met with great difficulties. The chief difficulty was that the government was in the hands of various religious authorities, and under their rule, the principles of exoteric religion prevailed. Therefore, those who sought attainment through the esoteric side of philosophy always had difficulty in speaking about it. Many were persecuted. They were stoned, they were flayed, they were put to death in many different ways. All sorts of punishments were inflicted upon them. Because of this, the progress of humanity was stunted. Today, we do not see as much of this; nevertheless, small mindedness with regard to religious and philosophical questions is to be found in all ages. The Sufis, by the help of meditation, found the source of knowledge in their own hearts; but it was very difficult to give it back to the world in plain words, even what little they could explain of the truth. The truth cannot really be spoken of in words, and yet, those gifted with poetic and prophetic expression have always had the inclination and tendency to express what their soul's have experienced.

Hafiz found a way of expressing the experiences of his soul and his philosophy in verse, for the soul enjoys expressing itself this way. The soul itself is music, and when it is experiencing the realization of divine truth, its tendency is to express itself in poetry. Therefore, Hafiz expressed his soul in poetry. And what poetry! Poetry full of light and shade, line and color—poetry full of feeling. No poetry in the world can be compared to that of Hafiz in its delicacy. Only the refined soul, with a subtle perception of light and shade expressed in words can grasp the meaning of the illumination of the soul. Nevertheless, the words of Hafiz have won every heart that has listened to them. Even those who do not wholly understand them are won by their rhythm, charm and beauty of expression.

In the East, the Persian language is considered the most delightful for poetry. It is soft, it is expressive, and its expression is tender. Every object has perhaps ten names for the poet to choose from, and the slightest thought can be expressed in some twenty different ways according to the poet's choice.

Hafiz, whose style resembles that of Solomon,

uses symbolism, such as the beloved's beautiful countenance in his poetry, her smiles, her glance, her graceful movements, the lover's feeling heart, his deep sigh, his pearl-like tears, the nightingale, the rose, the wine, the cup and the tavern, the arrow and the bow, spring and autumn. With these terms, he composed a special language in which to subtly express life's secret. All the other Persian poets, and also many of the poets of India, have adopted this terminology. Persian poetry is like painting; these poets painted pictures of the different aspects of life. The work of Hafiz, from beginning to end, is a series of beautiful pictures, ever-revealing and inspiring. Once a person has studied Hafiz, they have reached the top of the mountain from whence they behold the sublimity of the immanence of God.

The mission of Hafiz was to express to a fanatical religious world that the presence of God is not to be found only in heaven, but also here on earth. Often, religious belief in God and the hereafter has kept us asleep, waiting for that hour and day to come when we will be face to face with God, and many have seemed certain that that day would not come before death. Therefore, people have awaited death in the hope that they would see God in the hereafter, for heaven was the only place where God could be found. There was no other place, and no other way. In this way of thinking, only certain places, only churches are sacred places for worship, and God cannot be found anywhere else. The mission of Hafiz was to destroy this idea, and to make us conscious of the heaven close at hand, and to tell us that all we expect as a reward in the hereafter can be had here if we will only live a fuller life.

One of the principal teachings of Jesus Christ, an ideal that one also finds in other religions, is that "God is love." This was also the chief ideal of Hafiz, and he expresses it constantly in his *Dīvān*.[6] If there is anything divine in us, it is love. If God is to be found anywhere, it is in our hearts, and it is in love. And if love is awakened in the heart, then God is, so to speak, brought to life and born in us. But, at the same time, Hafiz has shown in his poetry that key to this is appreciation of beauty in all its forms.

Beauty is not always found in an object or a person. Beauty depends upon one's attitude to life, how one looks at it; and its effect depends upon our power of appreciation. The very same music, poetry, or painting will touch one person so that they feel its beauty to the very depths of their being, while another may look and see nothing special. The whole of manifestation has its beauty. Sometimes its beauty is clearly manifest to us, and sometimes we have to look for it. We may meet a good person, and be charmed by the beauty of goodness; but we may meet another person who seems bad, and yet, has good hidden in them somewhere, if we would only look for it, if only we had the desire to draw it out. The 'badness' is not always in the objects and persons, but often in our way of looking at them. The whole trend of the poetry of Hafiz is to awaken that appreciation and love of beauty that is the only means by which to experience that bliss which is the

---

6 *The New Testament*, 1 John 4:16.

purpose of our life.

Once, someone asked a Sufi the reason for this creation, and he answered, "God, whose being is love itself, desired to experience the nature of the divine Self; but, in order to experience it, God had to manifest and veil the divine being in order to discover the divine Self." God can be seen in all forms of nature, in all opposites—in the sun and the moon, in night and day, in male and female, in positive and negative—in order that the principle of love, itself the original and only principle behind the whole of manifestation, may play itself out. That is why the fulfillment of the purpose of life lies in the full expression of the love principle.

In learning philosophy, and looking at this world pessimistically, people have often renounced the world, calling it material and false. They have left the world, going off to forests, deserts, or caves, teaching the principle of self-denial and renunciation. But this was not the way of Hafiz. He said that life is like journeying over the sea and coming to a new land, a new port; before landing, we become frightened and say, "Perhaps I shall be attacked, or the place will attract me so much that I shall not be able to return to the place from whence I came." But, in saying this, it seems we have forgotten why we started out on that journey in the first place. We certainly did not undertake it in order to return without having landed somewhere. The attitude of Hafiz is to land, to risk it! If it turns out to be an attractive place, then he is ready to be won. If it will crush him, he is ready to be crushed. This is a daring attitude, not to run away from this false world, but to discover glimpses of the truth in it and to find God's purpose in the maze.

There is another great revelation which Hafiz brought to humanity in a most beautiful form. Many people in this world have, at one time, believed in God, in the divine mercy and compassion, in divine love and forgiveness; but, after witnessing catastrophes and injustice, or having suffered great sorrow, have given up their belief, have given up their religion. The reason for this is that the religion they followed taught them that God is Good, and God is Judge; and so they ask for justice from that Judge, but a justice to satisfy their own ideas. They think that their standard of justice is God's standard, and they look for goodness according to their understanding of it. Thus, a struggle arises in their hearts. They do not see justice because they are looking for it from their own point of view. They are looking for goodness, kindness, and mercy from their own point of view, and so see many situations which make them think that there is no justice and no such thing as forgiveness.

The way of Hafiz is different. The name of God is hardly found in the *Dīvān*. He does not express belief in God as the Just and the Good. His God is his Beloved, to whom he has surrendered in perfect love and devotion. Everything coming from the Beloved is accepted by him with love and devotion, as a reward. He prefers poison from the hand of the Beloved to nectar from the hand of another. He prefers death to life, if it is the wish of the Beloved.

One may ask, 'Is this fair?' There is no question of

'fairness' in love. Law is beneath love. Law is born of love. The mistake we make today is that we consider law to be higher than love. We do not see that the divine principle of love stands above law. Human beings make of God a judge who is bound by law, who cannot even act independently, but only according to what is written in a book. God is not justice. Justice is God's nature, but love is predominant. People attach such importance to actions and their results. They do not know that above action and result is a law which can consume the fires of hell, which can dominate even if the whole world were being drowned in the flood of destruction. They do not know that the power of love is greater than any other.

Think of the hen who takes care of her little ones. If they are threatened with danger, even if it should be a horse or an elephant, she fights because the principle of love is dominant. A kind mother is ready to forgive when her son comes home with head bowed, saying: "Mother, I have been so foolish. I have been insolent and have not listened to you. I am so sorry!" She is ready to understand and forgive him. So we see mercy and compassion is love, a stream of love that can purify all enmity and evil. And if a human being can forgive, why should God not forgive? Many dogmatic people in religions have taken away the love element that makes God sovereign. Instead, they make a God who is limited, who is bound by a book, and who cannot show compassion. If God were so limited, God could not be just. An individual would be better, because an individual can forgive.

The poetry of Hafiz has inspired the poets of Persia, as well as poets of India. The great Indian poet Rabindranath Tagore sometimes imparted a Persian color to his poems, and it is that color which has made them so popular.

Hafiz was one of ten disciples of a master, all of who were named Hafiz. Under the master's direction, he and the other disciples were expected to meditate together at a certain time of the night. One night, while he was in meditation, the master called out in his ecstasy, "Hafiz!" and our Hafiz came to the master immediately. The master blessed him with inspiration under the influence of his ecstasy, for at that moment, the master had achieved the ability to pass on the power of his own inspiration. That night, the master actually called out 'Hafiz!" ten times in his ecstasy, but each time, only our Hafiz responded to the call, because the other nine were sleeping and not meditating. Thus, our Hafiz received all ten blessings!

This is a symbolic story. The Inspirer is calling us from every direction, but we do not all respond. The voice is always there, the light is there, the guidance is there, but we are not always ready or willing to respond. We are not always open to the call. In reality, this is not only the story of Hafiz, but the story of every soul on earth.

Hafiz gives us a picture of human nature: hate, jealousy, love, kindness, vanity, the play of friendly impulse, the play of pride, and all aspects of life. Hafiz is not only a poet, but also a painter. He has made pictures of the different aspects of life. Every verse is a picture, and in every picture, whatever its 'color'—vanity, pride, conceit, love, mercy, or compassion in all their garbs—he sees only one spirit, the spirit of the Beloved. He shows the same devotion, appreciation and love to all the manifestations of that same Beloved.

He has insight into life and looks at it from a psychological point of view. However, at the same time, he sees the whole of life as the phenomenon of love, harmony and beauty, and recognizes all the different aspects of these. Whatever they are, he weaves them into a form so beautiful that it makes a wonderful picture.

From beginning to end, his phrasing is peculiar to himself. He uses words such as "wine," "goblet," and "beloved," and speaks of the "beautiful countenance of the beloved," the running river, the rising spring, the clear sky, the moon, the sun. In these poems, the lover continually reproaches the beloved. Then there is also the indifference of the beloved to all except her lover, so beautifully expressed that it almost seems as if while he was writing these poems the poet's soul was dancing. There is such musical inspiration that every line of his poetry is a strain of music.

The word "wine" is used often. According to the mystic, life itself is wine. To the mystic, each person drinks a particular wine. Hafiz pictures the whole world as a wine press, and every person partakes of that wine which is in accord with their own evolution. The wine of one is not the wine of another. He wishes to express the idea that every person—whether evolved or ignorant, whether honest or dishonest, whether they realize it or not, whether they have a great belief or no belief at all—is partaking of a certain wine. It is the type of intoxication produced by that particular wine that is their individuality, and when a person changes, they do so by drinking another wine. Every different kind of wine changes one's outlook on life; and every change in life is like partaking of a different wine.

Then Hafiz praises those who have come to a high realization. He says, "Be not fooled by the patched garment of the wandering dervish, for under the patched sleeves, powerful hands are hidden." He also says, "The bare-headed have a crown over their heads, if you only knew." By this he means that once a person has absorbed the thought of true reality, it not only ennobles their soul, but gives them a royal spirit. It is like being crowned. It is this inspiration and power which, in his poetry, he calls, "intoxication."

There are many religions and beliefs that tell us, someday, we will be able to communicate with God. But when will that day come? Life is so short, and our hearts are so hungry! If it does not come today, perhaps it will not come at all. Therefore, the thing Hafiz points-out from the beginning to the end of his work is this: "Do not wait for tomorrow; talk to the Beloved now! The Beloved is before you, here, in the form of your friend, in the form of your enemy, with a bowl of poison or with a rose. Recognize this and know it, for this is the purpose of life." Religions have made it seem like a journey of millions of miles, but Hafiz brings it close to hand.

We like complexity. We do not want to take just one step; it is more interesting to look forward to millions of steps. People seeking the truth get into a maze, and that maze is interesting. They want to go through it a thousand times. Like children, their whole interest is in running about; they do not want to see the door and go in until they are exhausted. So it is with adults too. They all say that they are seeking truth, but they love the maze. That is why the mystics made the greatest truths a mystery, to be given only to the few who were ready for them, letting the others play, because it was the time for them to play.

According to the Sufis, and all the prophets and sages who ever came to this world, love is the first principle, and also the last. In India, there are different kinds of *yoga* or 'discipline' that are practiced—some intellectual, some scientific, some philosophical, and some moral paths to God. However, the most desirable path to God that the Hindus have ever found—one which makes the whole of life beautiful—is *Bhakti Yoga*, the path of devotion, for it is the natural path. Our inclination is love. If we are cold, it is because we are in need of love. If we are warm, it is because love is alive. The only life, the very source of inspiration, salvation and liberation, is love.

Those great souls who have brought the Message of God to humanity—like the Buddha, Krishna, Jesus Christ, Moses, Abraham, or Zarathustra—were all learned. But whatever they learned, they learned from the love principle. What they knew was compassion, forgiveness, sympathy, tolerance, the attitude of appreciation, the opening of the heart to humanity. What they taught was love—a simple truth. If religions seem complex, they have added this complexity. In every case, what was brought by the prophets was simple, and was expressed in their personalities and their lives. It is that influence which has remained through the centuries after their passing. It is not the literature they left—most of that is from their disciples. It is the simple truth shown in their personalities, in their lives. The error of this time is that we cannot understand a simple truth, the truth as it is manifested everywhere. Instead, we try to find truth covered by a shell.

At the same time, Hafiz teaches one to see both the ultimate truth and the ultimate justice in God. He teaches that justice is not in related things, that perfect justice is in totality. He shows us that the power behind manifestation is the power of love, and that it is by this power that the whole world was created. It is the love principle, whether it works through God or through humanity. If that principle is behind the whole of creation, then it is this same principle that helps us to fulfill the purpose of our lives.

Hazrat Inayat Khan

Hazrat Inayat Khan was born in India in 1882. A master of Indian classical music, he gave up a brilliant career as a musician to devote himself full-time to the spiritual path. In 1910, he was sent into the West by his spiritual teacher and began to teach Sufism in the United States, England, and throughout Europe. For a decade and a half he traveled tirelessly, giving lectures and guiding an ever-growing group of Western spiritual seekers. In 1926, he returned to India and died there the following year. Today, his universalist Sufi teachings continue to inspire countless people around the world and his spiritual heirs may be found in every corner of the planet.

Made in the USA
Las Vegas, NV
17 June 2022

50346052R00042